The Goat in the Garden

retold by Linda B. Ross

illustrated by Stacey Schuett

❧ A Classic Tale ❧

Long ago, a farmer
and his wife
planted a garden.

One day, Goat went into the
garden. Goat ate the plants.

"Stop!" said the farmer
and his wife.

But Goat ate and ate.

"Let's get Dog,"
said the farmer.
"He will make Goat
go away."

So Dog went into the garden.
Dog barked at Goat.
But Goat kicked Dog
out of the garden.

"Let's get Duck,"
said the farmer's wife.
"She will make Goat
go away!"

So Duck went into the garden.
Duck quacked at Goat.
But Goat kicked Duck
out of the garden.

"Where is Cow?"
said the farmer.
"She will kick Goat out!"

So Cow went into the garden.
Cow mooed at Goat.
But Goat kicked Cow
out of the garden, too!

The farmer and his wife
were sad.
Soon they would have
nothing to eat!

"I can help," said a little ant.

"How can you help us?"
said the farmer and his wife.
"You are tiny!"

"Just watch!" said Ant.

Ant climbed up Goat's leg.
She bit Goat!

"Ouch!" cried Goat.

Ant climbed on Goat's back.
She bit Goat again and again!

"Ouch! Ouch!" cried Goat.
Then Goat ran out
of the garden!

Ouch!
Ouch!

"Thank you, little Ant!"
said the farmer and his wife.

"You are tiny, but you saved
our garden!"

"I like it here,"
said Ant.
"I will stay and
keep Goat away."

The Goat in the Garden

The Play

Characters

 Narrator

 Ant

Farmer

 Goat

 Wife

Narrator

Long ago, a farmer
and his wife
planted a garden.

One day, Goat went into
the garden. Goat ate
the plants.

 **Farmer** **Wife**

Stop!

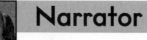 **Narrator**

But Goat ate and ate.

18

Farmer

Let's get Dog.
He will make Goat
go away.

 Narrator

So Dog went
into the garden.
Dog barked at Goat.
But Goat kicked Dog
out of the garden.

Wife

Let's get Duck.
She will make Goat
go away!

Narrator

So Duck went into
the garden.
Duck quacked at Goat.
But Goat kicked Duck
out of the garden.

Farmer

Where is Cow?
She will kick Goat out!

Narrator

So Cow went into
the garden.
Cow mooed at Goat.
But Goat kicked Cow
out of the garden, too!

The farmer and his wife
were sad.
Soon they would
have nothing to eat!

Ant

I can help.

 **Farmer** **Wife**

How can you help us?
You are tiny!

 **Ant**

Just watch.

 **Narrator**

Ant climbed up Goat's leg.
She bit Goat!

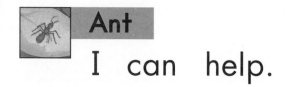 **Goat**

Ouch!

Narrator

Ant climbed on
Goat's back.
She bit Goat again
and again!

 Goat

Ouch! Ouch!

 Narrator

Then Goat ran out of
the garden!

Farmer   Wife

Thank you, little Ant.
You are tiny,
but you saved
our garden!

Ant

I like it here.
I will stay and
keep Goat away.